D1523172

Trees Don't Freeze

A Book About Adaptations

Thomas F. Sheehan

Rourke
Publishing LLC
Vero Beach, Florida 32964

www.rourkepublishing.com

PHOTO CREDITS: Title Page: © Galyna Andrushko; Page 04:© Vaida; Page 05: © Inger Anne Hulbaekdal; Page 06 © Giangrande Alessia; Page 07: © PhotoDisc, Inc.; Page 08: ©PhotoDisc, Inc.; Page 09: © Andrey Grinyov; Page 10: © Kris Butler; Page 11: © SaMBa; Page 12: © Jean Orrico; Page 13: © Till von Au; Page 14: © Danny Bailey; Page 15: © Mares Lucian; Page 16: © Les Delano; Page 17: © Kanwarjit Singh Boparai; Page 18: © Losevsky Pavel; Page 19: © Marcy Ugstad; Page 22: © Edyta Linek, Vladimir Ivanov

Editor: Robert Stengard-Olliges

Cover design by Michelle Moore.

Library of Congress Cataloging-in-Publication Data

Sheehan, Thomas F., 1939-
  Trees don't freeze : a book about adaptations / Thomas F. Sheehan.
     p. cm. -- (Big ideas for young scientists)
  ISBN 978-1-60044-537-8 (Hardcover)
  ISBN 978-1-60044-698-6 (Softcover)
1. Trees--Adaptation--Juvenile literature. I. Title.
  QK475.8.S44 2008
  581.4'2--dc22
                                     2007018566

Printed in the USA

CG/CG

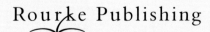

Rourke Publishing

www.rourkepublishing.com – rourke@rourkepublishing.com
Post Office Box 3328, Vero Beach, FL 32964

Table of Contents

What Is Adaptation?   4

Adaptation to Cold: Animals   8

Adaptation to Cold: Trees   12

Boreal Forests   14

Mountainside Trees   16

Tree Antifreeze   20

Glossary   23

Index   24

What Is Adaptation?

If a tree gets cold, what can it do? Can it pull on a jacket just like you?

Have you ever seen trees bundled in a
blanket of snow?

The ever-changing **weather** and **climate** of the Earth are a challenge to all living things.

Plants and animals have to adapt to survive. Especially when it is cold.

Adaptation to Cold: Animals

Some animals have thick fur for **insulation**, keeping their warmth in and the cold out. That's how polar bears survive in the Arctic.

Other animals **migrate** to avoid the wintery cold.

We have lots of ways to stay warm in the cold, too. What are some things you do to keep warm outside in the cold?

Trees can't do what people can do. What adaptations do you think trees have to survive in the cold?

Adaptation to Cold: Trees

Some trees curl up their leaves to save heat. Others drop their leaves in the fall and become **dormant**, like a sleeping bear.

Have you ever looked at the surface of leaves with a magnifying glass? You may have seen the furry-looking plant hairs on some of them. Furry leaves trap layers of air that insulate them.

Boreal Forests

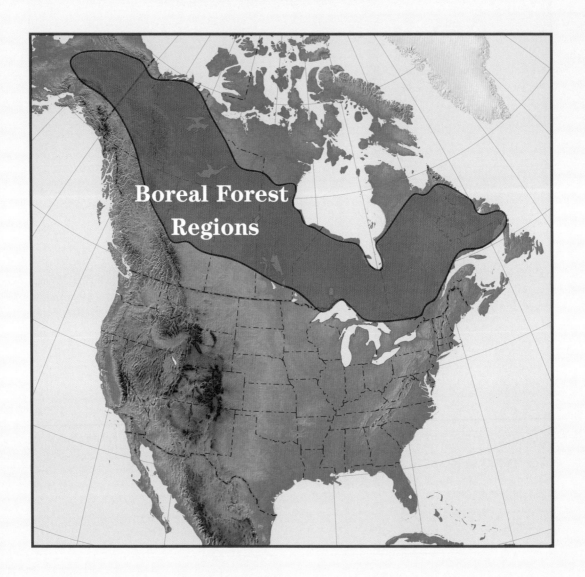

Boreal Forest
Regions

Evergreen trees in the northern Boreal forests have short, thick, dark green needles instead of wide, thin leaves. The darker needles can absorb more of the heat from the winter sunlight.

Spruce, hemlock, fir, and cedar trees have drooping branches that let snow slide off easily. This adaptation helps their needles get more winter sunlight and heat.

Mountainside Trees

On cold, windy mountainsides some trees grow in sheltered spots behind rocks and ledges, called out-crops. There, they avoid the wind-whipped cold.

Trees growing near the tops of mountains stay small and grow in nooks and crannies that protect them from freezing.

Have you noticed that your body gets used to the cold when you play outside in the winter?

Trees get used to the cold, too. We call these trees hardy trees.

Tree Antifreeze

How do trees adapt to the cold? First, water moves from the living parts of the tree to the non-living, woody parts. This prevents the water from freezing in the living parts and damaging, or killing the tree.

Then, if it gets even colder, the living part of the tree can make chemicals that act like **antifreeze**. The tree's antifreeze prevents the living parts from freezing and harming the tree.

Now, when you look outside on a cold winter day, you don't have to worry about shivering trees. Aren't you glad…that trees adapt to the cold so they don't freeze!

Glossary

adaptation (ad ap TAY shuhn) — a change that a living thing does so it fits better with its environment

antifreeze (AN tee freez) — a chemical that stops freezing

climate (KLYE mit) — the usual weather in a place

dormant (DOR muhnt) — showing no signs of action

insulation (IN suh lay shuhn) — material to stop heat from escaping

migrate (MYE grate) — to move from one region to another

organisms (OR guh nuz uhmz) — living plants or animals

weather (WETH ur) — the condition of the outside air

Index

adaptations   7, 11, 15, 20, 22

dormant   12

freezing   17, 20, 21, 22

heat   12, 14, 15

insulate   13

leaves   12, 13, 14

survive   7, 8, 11

winter   9, 14, 15, 18, 22

Further Reading

Glass, Susan. *Adaptation and Survival*. Perfection Learning, 2005.

Dahl, Michael. *Cold, Colder, Coldest: Animals That Adapt to Cold Weather*. Picture Window Books, 2006.

Parker, Steve. *Adaptation*. Heinemann Library, 2006.

Websites to Visit

www.sciencemadesimple.com/leaves.html

www.planetplant.org

About the Author

Thomas F. Sheehan is retired from 40 years of teaching elementary, middle, secondary, and post-secondary science. He is currently authoring science texts, which speak to children. Sheehan and his wife, Susan, reside on their farm in Mount Chase, Maine.